Gravity, 30.01.2025, Davide Macullo

ISPACE

THE ARCHITECTURE OF EMOTIONS

ORO Editions
Publishers of Architecture, Art, and Design
Gordon Goff: Publisher

EDIZIONI VRAWKA
Via Stradon 192, Rossa 6548, Switzerland

www.oroeditions.com
info@oroeditions.com

Published by ORO Editions

Authors: Davide Macullo, Philip Jodidio, and Valentina Perazzolo
Photographers: Corrado Griggi and Jung Ghim
Designer: Taylor Potecha
Project Manager: Jake Anderson

10 9 8 7 6 5 4 3 2 1 First Edition

ISBN: 978-1-966515-12-8

Prepress and Print work by ORO Editions Inc.
Printed in China

ORO Editions makes a continuous effort to minimize the overall carbon
footprint of its publications. As part of this goal, ORO, in association
with Global ReLeaf, arranges to plant trees to replace those used in the
manufacturing of the paper produced for its books. Global ReLeaf is an
international campaign run by American Forests, one of the world's oldest
nonprofit conservation organizations. Global ReLeaf is American Forests'
education and action program that helps individuals, organizations,
agencies, and corporations improve the local and global environment by
planting and caring for trees.

A WORLD THAT IS ALREADY THERE.
DAVIDE MACULLO IN ROSSA

Philip Jodidio
Lausanne, December 11, 2024

In Frank Capra's 1937 film Lost Horizon, a plane crashes in the Himalayas. Its passengers, who had been fleeing the turmoil of China, are led by Tibetans to the hidden valley of Shangri-la, where peace is a way of life, and the very process of aging has come to a halt. Based on a novel by James Hilton, Lost Horizon is merely one recent version of a story which recurs throughout the history of literature and art. It is the story of the Garden, of Paradise, lost and regained. The story remains symbolic of the search for meaning and understanding in a time when rapidity has all but overwhelmed contemplation.

The Val Calanca in the Italian-speaking region of the Canton of Graubünden (Switzerland) still brings to mind the image of a hidden paradise. Stretching about 25 kilometers from Roveredo in the south to Rossa in the north, it is a picture of idyllic mountain scenery which becomes more and more magical as visitors travel up its single access road. Rossa is located at 1,100-meters above sea level, not especially high as mountain villages go, but this valley and this town have an unexpected and rich history. The proximity of the Val Calanca to the San Bernardino Pass, which used to allow (or block) access from the north since the time of the Romans, places the area along a historic path leading from northern Europe to Italy.

In the 12th century, the neighboring valley of Mesolcina, which leads to the San Bernardino and Calanca, were inherited by the De Sacco family who resided in the castle of Mesocco. They ruled Calanca until 1480 when Giovanni Pietro De Sacco (Sax-Misox, 1452–1540) sold the territory to the Milanese warlord Gian Giacomo Trivulzio (1442–1518) who was then in the service of Ludovico (Il Moro) Sforza, Regent of Milan. In 1496, the area joined the so-called Grey League formed in what later became Graubünden. Following the French conquest of Milan in 1499, Louis XII appointed Trivulzio marshal of France, governor of the duchy, and marquis of

Vigevano in Lombardy. Trivulzio was thus recognized as a baron of the Grey League and a feudal lord of the King of France. The warlord's fame was such that he asked Leonardo da Vinci to design his tomb. Never realized, this grand equestrian monument survives only as a sheet of sketches (c. 1508) held today by the Royal Collection Trust. Trivulzio participated in the First Italian War of the newly crowned Francois I (1515–1516), when the French routed the combined forces of the Papal States and the Old Swiss Confederacy at Marignano in Lombardy in 1515 and captured Milan. The significance of this event is such that French school children still learn the date 1515 for "La Bataille de Marignan." As a consequence of their defeat, the following year, the thirteen Swiss Cantons signed a "perpetual" peace agreement with France in Fribourg and placed themselves in the service of the King of France, a status that they retained until the French Revolution. Trivulzio's star had faded in this period, and he died in France in 1518. His successor was his grandson Gian Francesco Trivulzio (1509–1573). The people of Mesolcina succeeded in buying their freedom from him in 1549.

This rather convoluted bit of history goes a long way to explaining the deeper nature of the Val Calanca and its inhabitants. Set near one of the major routes between northern and southern Europe, their fate was closely tied to the north while their language originated in Lombardy. As poor as it may have been in the 16th century and before, the mountain valleys near the San Bernardino Pass were a place of refuge from the sometimes-violent events that swept over the Alps. In 1803, Mesolcina and Calanca became part of the Swiss Confederation with the rest of Graubünden, and in 1818 a convention was signed between the King of Sardinia and Graubünden for the construction of the San Bernardino trade route.

A HISTORY MARKED BY THE CROSS

The protected nature of the Val Calanca is highlighted by the fact that the road into the valley was only built in 1830, and yet it is believed that almost 3,000 persons lived there in the 16th century. It is known in a more precise way that Rossa had a population of 450 persons in 1683. The rich history of the Val Calanca can in part be traced by its religious buildings, chapels, and churches that have withstood the test of time and that multiplied in the 17th century when individual villages were given permission to build their own places of worship by the church. The Parish Church of Santa Domenica, which is part of Rossa, was originally built in 1414 and considerably enlarged at the end of the 17th century. The parish church of the Assumption of St. Mary, first mentioned in 1219 was the center of the parish that at that time covered the entire valley. It is located in the village of the same name (Santa Maria) about seventeen kilometers south of Rossa at the entrance to the valley. The parish church of Rossa, dedicated to St. Bernard was built in 1677–1684. The parish also built several chapels in and around the same period: S. Carlo al Sabbione (painted by Francesco Antonio Giorgioli, 1694); S. Maria della Neve (1683, Valbella); S. Maria Maddalena al Calvario (1691); Madonna del Sangue and Madonna del Rosario (18th century); and S. Rocco (1725). Rossa became an independent municipality in 1851, having previously been part of Calanca. The landscape around Rossa is rugged and lined with trees, mostly larch. The chapels are placed to be visible, sometimes high above the town as is the case of the Cappella di Santa Maria Maddalena al Calvario, now seen with its wall paintings by David Tremlett.

A first interest in deeper study of the history of the town of Rossa, the highest village in the Val Calanca occurred in 2012 when the Calanca forestry official Orio Guscetti led a restoration effort to uncover, and repair terraced dry stone walls used for agriculture at the beginning of the 16th century in the area near the village called Scatta / Calvari. Now open to the public near paths that lead into the forest, the restoration of La Scatta might be considered the starting point of an adventure that has seen a generous transformation of Rossa into a place of art and culture.

PAINT THE TOWN RED

The Lugano-based architect Davide Macullo has played a significant role in this process. Although his family is from Rossa, Macullo's first project in the town was to build a weekend house for his brother in 1998, Swisshouse I. As the architect describes this project, which is directly influence by local vernacular architecture, "The atmosphere and the environment here are those typical of the Alps, where settlements have always grown with a careful and respectful approach to the rugged topography of the land and its resources." Inserted into the traditional terraced building system of the town, "The building," he says, "is intended to reinstate and, to an extent, enclose the space surrounding the church, defined in part by the existing houses." This early project of Macullo, the first completed by his architectural office is of interest because it demonstrates his attachment not only to Rossa as a place, but to its traditions and topography. This hamlet, with a population today of about 150 persons, is the unexpected focus of the RossArte Foundation, whose goal is to promote contemporary art and sustainable economic and cultural growth, thus

"increasing the cultural public heritage of the Calanca valley." Macullo created RossArte in 2017 in collaboration with the town's mayor (Graziano Zanardi), the local urban planner (Ivano Fasani), and the founder of the Galleria Continua Mario Cristiani, as artistic director.

IN THE WORDS OF THE ARCHITECT

In December 2024, Davide Macullo explained how he went on to create his own house in Rossa with the artist Daniel Buren and to begin to imagine a series of artistic interventions in the town, culminating with his Ispaces, eight relatively small wooden structures erected along local forest paths with the goal of giving visitors a sense of wayfinding in every sense of the word. These structures express a real, engaged and engaging vision of the purposes and future of architecture.

What is your own family's relation with the town of Rossa?

My family arrived there in the late 17th century. More than a century ago, after completing middle school, the people of Rossa began to frequently go to Zurich. My grandfather, his brothers, and his children—including my father—left the village looking for more opportunities in Zurich and Geneva, as well as in Canada and across Europe. The relationship between my family and Rossa has always been one of simultaneous distance and care. Even though they rarely returned, they always took care of the territory of Calanca, making donations for the church's restoration, for example. My one uncle who remained in Rossa was the mayor of the village for thirty years.

Where did you spend time in Rossa?

Each of my family members owned a house in Rossa, and each used to stay there on holidays. When I was a child, my parents built a chalet to spend holidays there, but since they were busy with their restaurant we rarely visited. I did not grow up in Rossa, but in Giornico, in Ticino, which is about fifty kilometers away. The first new project built by my office was a house for my brother in Rossa, when I was still a student. It was intended to be a weekend house but became his permanent residence, where he moved at a certain age. When he got close to retirement, we built another house for him nearby: a refurbishment with an extension, where his son is currently living.

Did you personally spend your holidays in Rossa as an adult?

I didn't spend my holidays in Rossa, but when I was looking for a house in the mountains with my family, particularly for the children, we chose to build it in Rossa.

You designed that house in collaboration with the French artist Daniel Buren. Why is that?

When I was a teenager, I was in love with the work of Buren. My passion was conceptual art. In fact, I wanted to be a conceptual artist. I observed his ability to express everything through colored lines, and that gave me courage to go on and to believe in abstract thinking and abstract art.

How did you reach out to Daniel Buren and the other artists?

Buren was working with Studio d'Arte Contemporanea Dabbeni in Lugano. For years, Felice Dabbeni gave me art lessons. He was a brilliant man. Thanks to the Dabbeni Studio we were also able to contact David Tremlett. I met him in Lugano. We went to lunch with the collectors and friends Heidi and Klaus Schwab, and we decided to visit the churches. He came up to Rossa and we asked him to paint one of the churches in the village. To begin working with Daniel Buren, I went to the founder of Galleria Continua, Mario Cristiani, and he connected us. Buren was enthusiastic about working on my house, and for me that was a dream.

You changed your plans early in your life. After wanting to be an artist, you went into architecture.

After hundreds of projects, I realized that architecture is the most complete of the arts, and our current research goes into conceptual thinking. That was my starting point.

When I decided not to be an artist but an architect, I still dreamt of making a collection of art and designing a building for it in Rossa. Eventually though, I concluded that art had become too commercial. I visited art fairs for more than thirty years, but I lost all pleasure in that activity. I thought, "Why should I have a private collection when the valley is like a home?" When I walk out the door, I'm still in my garden, even if I run in the valley and I swim in the river. So, the idea of creating artworks in Rossa developed along the lines of the thought of the artist and designer Bruno Munari: "Civilized people live amidst their art, their own art." Imagine being at home, looking out of the windows, and seeing art everywhere. So, the collection had to be public and not private. It became less of a burden and more about sharing. For the Rossa Project, after Daniel Buren, I contacted the Swiss artist Niele Toroni, who is living in Paris, but unfortunately, he could not come. My house was underway in 2016; the same year I contacted David Tremlett. The whole idea is not to spread art around, but to have art-as-urban-fabric for citizens to enjoy.

What of the style of these artists? All are hard-edge abstractionists—Buren with his straight lines, Toroni with dots, Tremlett with rather angular but very abstract forms. Is this a specific style you are drawn to?

Yes. I think, first, these artists are all connected in some way. In terms of a curatorial way of building up an environment, the choice of Buren and Tremlett was very personal. I love Tremlett's positive way of looking at life. He was perfect for Rossa because his work is about enhancing the peculiarities of a place through his paintings.

I understand that you like this kind of abstraction which is hard-edged, certainly for Tremlett and Buren. How

does that relate to a wild place like Rossa for you?

I believe that these artists can synthesize the beauty of nature. They have the power to take the essential and reduce every complex aspect to the minimum. I contacted the Swiss artist Felice Varini to work on a wall in the town, along with Stuart Arend, another artist that I love. He also works in abstract forms related to buildings and place. I think that his work and approach are in harmony with Buren and Tremlett, and he deserves a space in Rossa's art as well.

The art that you choose is a personal preference, but you told me that you really didn't have opposition from people in the village to any of this. Were there some who didn't like it?

First, it's important to stress that the Rossa Project is a collective effort, where everyone involved contributes to make this vision reality. Much of my engagement in Rossa was about spending the most possible time there, to chat and get to know people. I spent so much time with them just to make them feel comfortable and closer to the idea of enhancing the urban fabric through art. They also got to know and appreciate the artists. This made people from Rossa become confident about the seriousness of art. When I first started with this idea of putting art in Rossa, I went to meet the mayor Graziano Zanardi. We didn't know each other well, but he knew my family. From the very beginning, he was comfortable with my ideas and gave me confidence and great support. Everything here is about contributing to social life with joy.

How do you explain that there has been no opposition to the idea of having abstract paintings in several locations in an old mountain village?

Rossa is actually a cosmopolitan place. All people there speak at least two, sometimes three languages. Everybody has a history of emigration. Rosanna, who is now a farmer in Rossa, spent her working career in Zurich, speaking German, French, and Italian. At fifty, she chose to be a farmer in Rossa, and she now lives there, with her fifty goats that we all love. These fantastic people are very open and brilliant. Rossa has quite a diaspora. Many people from the village are currently living all over the world—in Canada, Argentina, the United States, and Australia, but they still feel they belong to the Calanca Valley. For example, when we have elections the majority of them comes back to Rossa to vote or at least participate through mail-in voting.

How did you come to the concept of the Ispaces?

It's related to the idea of enhancing and promoting the destiny of the valley. I studied the psychology of space in art school. When I decided to realize this project, together with Lorenza Tallarini and Aileen Forbes-Munnelly, Michele Tedeschi—who studied at art school with me—appeared at the office and was of great help in the research on psychology needed to deepen the basis for the Ispaces. Together with Lorenza, my partner in the studio, we have been saying for years that we should try to explore this subject more deeply in an abstract form. Then, we chose Rossa to start implementing our studio's

approach. We chose the woods of Rossa because so many trees were being cut, so in a way we tried to adapt our ideas to a more sustainable approach. The people, the mayor, the parish, and the forest ranger liked the idea so much that they enthusiastically allowed us to realize our project alongside theirs. So, we did it.

The Ispaces are all made with local wood, and they are quite small. Why is that?

The size of the Ispaces is determined by human size: they occupy about thirty square meters. They were designed based on the capacity of bodies to fill a space and what people can comfortably manage. They're spaces that you can still feel with your body, with your senses. The dimensions were also determined by optimizing the relationship between the size of the trees and the cuts, ultimately arriving at the dimensions of the beams. A rational approach was developed through collaboration aimed at keeping costs close to zero, which reflects the soul of the Rossa Project, which was based on volunteer work.

Are these structures meant to be permanent?

Ispaces don't have large foundations. They are supported by screw-like piles that can be removed without disturbing the natural setting. The structures have a normal lifespan of around twenty years: when they get older, the mass and integrity of the wood decreases. But you can still restore them. The wood can be used in other construction, or the Ispaces can be rebuilt using the original foundations. It is about structures that are integrated into nature and the surroundings, that follow the natural course of their environment.

The project has evolved since the first concept was developed I believe?

Our first intention was to create ten Ispaces. We started with Jung Kim—a young artist from Seoul—Aileen, and Lorenza, designing about thirty different structures, and then selected eight of them instead of ten. With the extra wood we later decided to create the Temples of Thought: three are in Rossa, one in Tesserete, and one in Tirana, Albania. These structures are intended to be built around the world with different partners, artists, and architects. The idea is that they feel free to draw inspiration from a fruit, flower, or natural element native to their country—something related to the use of typical materials with the help of local artisans. This new initiative began years ago in Rossa supported by Maria Elena Rudolf and Florin Mindirigiu, the curators of the Temple of Thought. We now have many projects for temples around the world, with Rossa at the center of a global network of projects dedicated to the human capacity of producing abstract thought.

You have worked with Valentina Perazzolo on the psychological implications of the Ispaces. I find that this analysis may not be immediately obvious to visitors. What do you really hope to achieve with the Ispaces in a more general way? To make people aware of the psychology of architecture? Is that the goal?

Yes. The communication of our projects goes through many layers. I always say that if I explained every idea we put in a project to clients they would fire me because it would be too much—too heavy, sometimes too philosophical. What clients expect from us is to deliver a building that impresses, a building that is beautiful, a building that expresses something. We transform the requested necessities into opportunities.

The Ispaces are a good example of layers of understanding in architecture. This is what they are really about. They simplify the complex process of designing and explain our studio's main pillars. The first layer of interpretation is about discovery. Visitors are invited— even compelled—to enter the forest and explore the surroundings. Moreover, the project is part of a territorial revaluation, as it contributes to the restoration of the old paths and parts of the forest. The goal is to attract visitors and enrich a rural Swiss village with beautiful wooden structures that people love for their essence. And then there is another layer—sociability. Creating a convivial community space means giving visitors the possibility to talk with others. Not only this, the Ispaces allow the organization of group intergenerational activities such as yoga, dance workshops, and more. What is nice is that when you cross paths with people in the forest, you normally just greet them, but when you have a place to rest you can truly talk and connect. Creating a place devoted to sociability is always an achievement. Finally, the Ispaces allow us to connect with our inner selves, apart from social interactions. The sculptures serve as spaces that encourage individual exploration, fostering a connection with nature and our soul.

But your real intentions go beyond that conviviality, don't they?

Our intention was to show people that the spaces we live in can have an impact on our moods and feelings. If I enter a space with angles, it can stimulate aggressiveness, whereas round forms have a softer impact. A space can transmit a feeling: aggression, calm, stability, or even a sense of freedom. The Ispace called Clessidra (Hourglass), for example, has an open view toward the sky. The air and views go up, drawning one toward the sky. You fly, in a way. The Pyramid is like fire. It makes you feel vulnerable in an unwelcoming place. We cut the wood with sharp angles so that they could be threatening. The cube, with windows and "walls," generates a feeling of familiarity, stability, and tranquility. A tree is planted in it though, which raises the question, "Is the cube the house of the tree, or mine? Am I the guest or is it the tree?" Ispaces are physically off the main paths, out of the comfort zone of visitors. This encourages them to walk, explore, and feel the forest.

For those who become interested in the psychology of space, how do you approach their visits?

The deeper you go, the more you can find literature on the psychology and perception of space. The library we plan to create in Rossa will, of course, have books about these subjects. We are also planning to hold a summer seminar for architects on the psychology of space. I believe this subject is important for the next generation of architects. In the future, houses will be designed in laboratories and built with 3D printers. The architect of the future will need to care about the well-being of residents. I believe the psychology of space is the future of the profession. And this is, in fact, what interests me.

You have expressed your interest in the psychology of space in many of your other projects.

Yes, in all our projects every line is drawn with a purpose, aiming to create an aesthetic rooted in the perception of its users. One example of the application of these psychological principles is the Swisshouse XXXIV in Galbisio (2017). We designed it starting from a cube. Then, we developed it dynamically, opening it toward the outside while still maintaining its cubic essence. Inside the house, you feel stable and protected, yet simultaneously projected toward the exterior. As a teenager, I dreamed of being a conceptual artist. One of the projects I sketched in my little notebook involved setting concrete slabs in the field to define space and to explore the relation between interior and exterior. In this house, we were able to realize that concept. Concrete slabs extend in all directions creating a connection between inside and outside—so clear that windows almost seem unnecessary. If the windows were removed, the house would still retain its meaning. This concept is also related to the history of architecture and Mondrian's Neo-plasticism, further grounding the design in a broader artistic and theoretical framework.

Isn't the psychology of space what the history of architecture is about? Some buildings, one might think first of the Italian Renaissance, just make the visitor feel at ease. Even if there was

no medical study of physical reactions, somehow architects knew about some of the psychological effects that you refer to. Vastu shastra in India and feng shui are perceived by some as the rules of architecture relating to well-being.

The psychology of space goes beyond history. It unites past, present, and future. We don't just design and build thinking in three dimensions: we design with the idea that architecture needs to be thought about in time, especially for the generations to come. To inhabit a space means to live in it, and a space is truly lived in, in time. Time is the fundamental component in the creation of a space, and the image of a project is simply its consequence. What truly changes from one era to another is not so much technology or its impact on our understanding of space, but rather the way we perceive a space and its rhythms of use. In fact, it is the timing of spatial perception that shifts with our evolving habits, tied to human mobility and the routines of everyday life.

What are some examples of architecture that has moved you?

There are buildings and places that have touched me deeply: Fatehpur Sikri in India (1569), the Tomb of Agamemnon in Greece (c.1400–1250 BCE), the Temple of Heaven in China (1420), the San Carlo Church alle Quattro Fontane (1644, Borromini), and the Pazzi Chapel in Florence (1478, Brunelleschi). When you visit these places, you perceive a completely comfortable space, because the proportions are well conceived. I am studying anthropology because it helps me understand the motivations behind human choices and, of course, their

errors. There are some very deep-seated human concerns that must be addressed in spaces, such as the fear of being trapped. Starting from ancestral feelings like this, we approach design with a particular touch, always considering a clear escape route. I have worked in Korea, China, and India, so I am familiar with feng shui and vastu shastra. The Ispace is not a finished product. It is not something that tells you the end of a story. Instead, it is the beginning of something.

Are the Ispaces sculpture or architecture, or both?

Sometimes I find it difficult to call myself an architect. Some art, music, or words can be eternal, can endure longer than architecture, which is more directly subject to the wearing element of time. Moreover, architecture does not exist if nobody enters it. A picture is not evocative enough to be able to make you feel architecture. With architecture you can really realize everything. Sculpture and architecture for me are the same thing. I don't really make a distinction between them. I don't really define myself as an architect. In the studio, we have fun generating elements from our imagination, playing with mood, psychology, and materials as though they are the ingredients that can be combined together to cook a delicious dish. We aim to create places for people, rather than just to build spaces.

IN ANCIENT TRADITIONS

The words of Davide Macullo and of Valentina Perazzolo found elsewhere in this book offer an introduction to the Ispaces. As they explain, these forms play not only on architecture, structure, and proportions but also on psychology. These are not pure and simple forms but are developed from spherical, pyramidal or spiral templates. At first glance, some bring to mind drawings like Leonardo da Vinci's Pyramis laterata pentagona vacua, first published in Luca Pacioli's treatise Divina Proportione, (Venice, 1509). Pacioli considered three-dimensional geometry in its divinely human and natural expression in the light of Plato's Timaeus, written in about 360 BCE, which assigns specific forms to the basic elements: "Let us give earth the cubical shape, since of the four kinds, the earth is the most immobile and most plastic of all bodies and that which has the most stable bases must necessarily be like her…Of the rest, water is the most immobile, fire the most mobile, and air is the intermediate between the two; we shall assign the smallest body [tetrahedron] to fire, the largest [icosahedron] to water, and the intermediate [octahedron] to air; and the sharpest to fire, the next to air, and the third to water." The idea that a geometric (thus potentially architectural) form can be assigned a unique correspondence to one of the four main elements of nature speaks to the deep and ancient concept of an underlying order, a mathematical underpinning of what today we might call the psychology of space.

THE VERY KERNEL OF ITS EXISTENCE

Reference to color, or the connection between forms and color, does not spring only from recent scholarly studies either. It is something deeply ingrained in our psyche that words cannot adequately reflect what each person may feel (or not). Explaining the emotional meanings of color, in his book Concerning the Spiritual in Art (1911), Wassily Kandinsky wrote, "It is clear that all I have said of these simple colors is very provisional and general, and so also are those feelings (joy, grief, etc.) which have been quoted as parallels of the colors. For these feelings are only the material expressions of the soul. Shades of color, like those of sound, are of a much finer texture and awake in the soul emotions too fine to be expressed in words. Certainly, each tone will find some probable expression in words, but it will always be incomplete, and that part which the word fails to express will not be unimportant, but rather the very kernel of its existence."

So too, the symbolic meanings of architecture, sometimes obvious and on other occasions far more subtle, escape scientific explanation, they are felt, or they are not. In The Dynamics of Architectural Form (1975), Rudolf Arnheim wrote, "The cupola of a dome may no longer signify a religious image of heaven; but as an overarching and surrounding hollow, it forever preserves a spontaneous affinity with the natural sky and shares some of its principal expressive connotations." Arnheim and others have also looked deeply into what might be called the meanings of color. In his treatise Art and Visual Perception (1954), Arnheim effectively questions any scientific study of the psychological impact of colors, or rather the mechanism by which color generates feelings:

Nobody denies that colors carry strong expression, but nobody knows how such expression comes about. To be sure, expression is widely believed to be based on association. Red is said to be exciting because it reminds of fire, blood and revolution. Green calls up the refreshing thought of nature and blue is cooling like water. But the theory of association is no more illuminating here than it is in other areas. The effect of color is much too direct and spontaneous to be only the product of an interpretation attached to the precept of learning... On the other hand, we have not even a hypothesis to offer about the kind of physiological process that might account of the influence of color.

INTO THE VOID

It would not be a foreign idea to Davide Macullo that some of the most radical ideas of modern architecture have been conceived by artists. The Frenchman Yves Klein published a brief text in 1958 called The Monochrome Adventure. He dared to imagine a "new architecture" that is based on atmosphere "that cannot be seen or touched." Color, like the shade of blue that he favored, would infuse and inhabit this space. "For me," he wrote, "the colors are living beings, highly evolved individuals who integrate themselves to us and to everything. Colors are the true inhabitants of space." His was an ode not to solidity, but to the void, which could only be attained by leaping into it, as he dared to suggest in the 1960 photo Saut dans le vide, where he appears to be diving or hovering one floor above a Paris street.

Drawing attention to the psychological or even physiological impact of architectural forms is the ultimate goal of the Ispaces, but this means that it is about giving form to the unknowable, or that which cannot be stated in words.

In fact, it is surely better to simply feel these spaces than to try to explain them. They are about what might be termed the "missing" dimension of architecture, more properly the dimension which was always there but which has often been ignored in modern times. Call it the dimension of the spirit, or of the essence of things, it is situated in a place that remains forcibly undefined. That place may be precisely the void that Yves Klein leapt into with his "Air Architecture," or maybe it resides in eight unexpected wooden pavilions in the forest near Rossa. Davide Macullo rightly says that the Ispaces are intended to be read in different ways. Why not see them as a pleasant destination for a Sunday walk, a discovery by the side of a forest path, shapes that might be as much related to antiquity as they are to the modern world.

The Ispaces have neither windows nor doors in the traditional sense. In fact, they serve no discernable purpose except in offering a place to meet. They have neither electricity nor running

water. The American sculptor Richard
Serra said, "The difference between art
and architecture is that architecture
serves a purpose." Perhaps agreeing
in this case with Serra, Davide Macullo
says that he sees no difference between
architecture and art. Perhaps with the
Ispaces he touches on something close
to the minimalism he so much admires
in the work of Buren and Tremlett: "They
take the essential and reduce everything
to the minimum," he says. Macullo
takes the earth, wind, and rain of the
forest and creates small structures
that are free and open, but which
almost inevitably challenge visitors
to question themselves. The French
phenomenological philosopher Maurice
Merleau-Ponty (1908–1961) wrote, "I
create an exploratory body dedicated
to things and to the world, of such
sensitivity that it invests me to the most
profound recesses of myself and draws
me immediately to the quality of space,
from space to the object, and from the
object to the horizon of all things, which
is to say a world that is already there."[1]

HORIZONS, LOST AND FOUND

And what if the Lost Horizon of the 1937 film, the Shangri-la of a modern world in search of meaning were to be found in the hills of Rossa. The apparently almost gratuitous gesture of a native of this small village has been to fashion unexpected wooden pavilions and to leave them open and free. The Ispaces may be shared with other visitors or sometimes experienced alone, but for those who pause and feel, there is something in these otherwise empty volumes. Not as much places to view nature as to be in nature, be part of a forest that speaks of centuries of human habitation and eons of evolution. The Ispaces are not about anything tangible, though their volumes are enveloping, and, for the most part, protective. They are about what cannot be explained but must be felt. It is entirely up to the visitor to enter, to look up or to close their eyes, but finally for some, to perceive the "horizon of all things, which is to say a world that is already there."

ROSSA AND THE CALANCA VALLEY **BETWEEN PAST AND FUTURE**

Davide Macullo

When I enter the valley and close the door behind me, a world of dreams and visions opens. This is a an unpolluted, healthy, genuine, and vibrant place, one that is human-sized, uplifted by the magnificence of nature. We still belong to nature, even if during centuries we strived, with sense of often unhealthy pride to distance ourselves from it. The Calanca Valley today offers a refuge and laboratory, open to people sensitive to the future of living, or more precisely, for those seeking the ideal place to live in harmony between genuine progress and nature. Inspired by the philosophical notes of the Italian designer and artist Bruno Munari (1907–1998), who referred to "a civilized people live in the midst of their own art," we seek to build a place made of reasons to exist and coexist with the elements. We recognize nature's dominant role and set aside the idea that we are the main drivers of the natural destiny of things.

We have reached a turning point that represents an unprecedented, epochal rupture that it is wise to recognize before we suffer the full consequences. The break with the ancient era, including the brief period called modern/contemporary, from the 1500s to today, will expand dramatically with the advent of artificial intelligence. As historically experienced by the majority of people, adaptation to rapid change represents a challenge, especially when these changes erase certainties acquired during all of recorded history. Change started with the advent of agriculture, which shaped human destiny until yesterday and, I hope, it will again shape the future in a suitable way.

Mutations in ecology in a broad sense (climate, politics, the economy) and human ecology (moods) already challenge people to be faithful to their own purpose, which is to say to the voice of consciousness within each person, to paraphrase Pope Francis. The distortions caused by globalization caught many unprepared, accentuating the between different parts of the population—

the poor and the wealthy, the young
and the old. Feelings of inadequacy
related to the new rhythms of life have
exacerbated misunderstandings and
damaged the delicate mechanisms
of education and the transmission of
values from one generation to the next.
Culture, when it can be isolated from
obsolete conventions and inevitable
corruption, still represents a precious
tool that generates comprehension
between generations. It remains the key
to building a healthy society that permits
the development of a healthy society,
that allows humans to inhabit the planet
in a genuine, sustainable way.

Rossa and the Calanca Valley represent
the potential for an ideal microcosm
that embodies the flame of a renewed
intergenerational dialogue, based in
a natural setting that expresses an
overwhelmingly rich environment
compared to the presence of man.
A place where the presence of the
geological time scale makes it possible
to remember and reflect on the brevity
of life, and on the utility of adding a
constructive element in the service of
humanity's future. For the moment,
this place is far from armed conflict,
which is the ultimate expression of
the misunderstandings that can be
overcome through love for what we have
inherited. Each person is in a position
to comprehend the exceptional nature
of this historic moment, and to act in
a proactive way to trace the path to
be taken. The citizens of this valley
have attained a degree of freedom that
has avoided the need for excessive
assistance, and they are aware of
the value of the liberty that they have
achieved.

We must imagine a house that is built with patience and collaboration. A house that will shelter humanity from the injustices we inflict on ourselves if we remain indifferent to changes. The Ispace project is inserted as a fundamental element in the thought process that we dedicate to the two forms of ecology. The first, in a broad sense, is an implicit commitment to caring for the land, and the second is the research essential to help people recognize the importance of feeling comfortable in built space. Each of us inhabits space and we often suffer from it, precisely because the spaces we create are not designed with the necessary sensitivity to fulfill their essential task: to make people feel at ease and allow for the development of abilities aimed at improving living conditions with a healthy development toward the future. Man has always sought ideal space, but this search has been slowed by human nature itself. This failure is due to the preference given to short-term motivations linked to opportunistic needs and feelings.

Ispace is a concrete expression of an artisanal ecological laboratory. It is sophisticated in its calibration of the concepts of space and place that are necessary to finally stop building spaces and start creating places. An awareness of the delicacy of human feelings can be realized in the construction of a habitat that accommodates shared psychological characteristics, continuously adapting to the most advanced technology. The construction of the new world starts from within, expressing itself with neither prejudice nor any will to dominate what lies beyond. We must live both inside and outside of ourselves.

ISPACES:

A NEUROARCHITECTURAL JOURNEY THROUGH MIND, BODY, AND SOUL

Valentina Perazzolo

ONLY A DIFFERENT EXPERIENCE OF ART CAN SAVE US FROM DEHUMANIZATION

Ispace is a significant project, encapsulating deep psychosocial implications within aesthetically simple structures. These forms symbolize a transformative shift, challenging rooted beliefs and concepts not only in arts and architecture but also in broader fields. It signifies a shift that encompasses a wider scope of human sciences, particularly within society. Architecture possesses the potential to impact social issues, collective behavior, and cognitive processes across time. It is firmly rooted in place and culture.

Given that people are intrinsically social, their understanding of the world thrives on relational potential. Following this notion, intersubjectivity can be linked to intercorporeality.[2] Empathy, compassion, emotional cognition, and exchange are not solely confined to the human sensory sphere; they arise from interactions and coordination between motor and sensory worlds, profoundly influencing human experience.

Consequently, we are continuously shaped by the environment around us, to the extent that our adaptive organism is the result of changes prompted by environmental shifts. The brutalization and alienation of our environment have contributed to the dehumanization of modern cities, leading to a pandemic of mental and physical illnesses. These consequences arise from a world built for objectives that have diverged from fundamental human needs. Notably, architecture often overlooks temporal considerations, focusing primarily on spatial aspects. This paradox becomes evident when considering that human experience evolves through time and actions.

IS PACE – È PACE, I SPACE – IO SPAZIO, IS PACE – È RITMO

Ispace is about architecture that speaks a universal language, an effective simplexity[3] that gives prior relevance to humanity and its intimate essence. The project consists of two different aspects working in parallel: primarily a level of expression, defined by the concrete development of shapes and substance that generate an aesthetic simplicity within everyone's comprehension; and, on the other side, the level of content extends to the abstract and complex essence that—extracted from the shapes— reveals profound meanings with strong ideological and cultural value.

More specifically, Ispace and the entire Rossa project seek to bring individuals closer to the origin of everything and divert them from the artificiality of the modern built world. This project aims to bring people closer to fundamental nature, reasserting primary needs and reevaluating scales of value. An explorative path leads the user to experience the three steps of perception, both emotionally and cognitively, within the space and the experience. Wood offers the opportunity for a reflective perception, generated by an active and conscious stimulation of one's body and senses. Ispace, on the other hand, provides the chance to reflect on interiority in a visceral, instinctual, and emotive way, drawing sensations from the architecture. Before entering the structures, the sensorial, perceptual path is actively opened, driven by natural curiosity to explore the wooded environment. Once inside the structures, however, this process takes a backseat and becomes autonomous, prioritizing a deeper and conscious investigation of interiority. It's a path that starts from an exteroceptive[4] approach, an interaction between body and space, seamlessly transitioning into a proprioceptive[5] state characterized by consciousness of one's own being, posture, and body movement.

EMOTIONS DRAW SPACES: GROWTH SHOULD ALSO BE SUSTAINABLE, ESPECIALLY IN HUMAN SPIRITUAL TERMS

The concept of ritual within the project is rooted in envisioning the space as a dedicated haven for a specific experience of relaxation and meditation. The process involves exploring one's inner self, fostering mindfulness through the activation of fronto-limbic[6] networks. This activation facilitates emotional regulation, reducing stress levels and cultivating a state of mental tranquility. This transition occurs by reducing retention and alertness, essential for conceptualizing the space as an entity to synchronize with. Nature plays an indispensable role in this process, as it stimulates attention and reduces blood pressure, cardiac activity, and anxiety, aiding in introspection. This outcome is achievable only if users can anticipate the space's reactions to their actions and movements, transcending mere self-awareness, a phenomenon known as affordances.[7]

Architecture that enables users to create affordances considers the essential essences and physiological sensations experienced by users during the design phase. The construction of peripersonal space[8] depends on the encoding of actions; motor acts within this space form a sphere for potential action around us. Perception isn't solely passive but involves an interplay with cognition and action. This necessitates that the body and mind undergo a suspension and redirection of attention, embracing a mode of receptivity, also known as *epoché*.[9] Each emotion attended to is matched with a dynamic sensorimotor[10] pattern.

ARCHITECTURE SHOULD NOT REQUIRE INSTRUCTIONS TO BE EXPERIENCED BUT SHOULD OFFER A NATURAL SENSE OF ORIENTATION.

Essential geometries have been conceived in an ideasthetic[11] context, associated with concretized sensations that later evoke behavioral reactions. As Erwin Straus[12] asserted, all forms of human behavior managed by the motor system can be directly linked to their metaphorical extension. The subject is thus architecture that moves away from the mere idea of form to become habitat, a structure of consciousness, and also action: the form is a verb, inviting a human regression to the essence of breathing, resonating, dancing, and touching. Dynamic and living architecture, where shapes extend upwards, inviting visitors to explore dimensions of space and time with their body and mind, playing with their posture, body, and head positions, which define the experience. Architecture capable of influencing sensations and moods.

The choice to represent emotions through geometric shapes is not arbitrary. Gestalt[13] formalizes the theory of spatial perception where the mind recognizes images within shapes. Perception, therefore, is a process of mental construction and shapes, more than color, which influence the emotions perceived within virtual architecture.

The project originates from the synesthetic[14] translation of emotional states into essential forms—cube, pyramid, and sphere—considering focal points concerning the world of architecture and perception. Indeed, cubes and spheres are associated with stability, familiarity, and balance. Curves elicit positive emotions and motivation, determined by an innate perceptual reaction triggered by the activation of the occipito-temporal cortex and visual cortex. If curves represent a universally shared and recognized preference, the repetition of strong, sharp lines and edges induces amygdala[15] activation and, consequently, an aversion to perceived danger.

Shapes, but also the presence of harmonic proportions, perceived through multisensory integration contribute to the effectiveness of design and elements such as wayfinding, rhythm, and embodiment.[16] The clarity of escape routes facilitated by the continuity between inside and outside defies the conception of space as a delimited and closed entity. A sense of enclosure would induce further perception of danger, consequently activating the anterior mid-cingulate cortex and increasing production of the stress regulating hormone cortisol. This absence of obstacles makes the Ispace project aesthetically understandable, intuitive, and thus capable of accompanying the processes of catharsis and introspection. The pure presence of nature and light refers to their emblematic evolutionary function, today also known to be therapeutic. Natural light regulates hypothalamic inputs, reduces cortisol levels by inhibiting melatonin secretion, and regulates the circadian rhythm. Its dynamism also generates movement within structures, creating architectures present not only in space but also in time.

Nature, understood as biodiversity, can contribute to the reduction of the toxicity of stress, anxiety, and the cognitive overload of daily life, providing physical and mental recovery. Stimulating motor activity, social contact, and cohesion immediately induces a positive emotional response. Nature is present in the construction materials, allowing a continuity with the surrounding forest environment. The porosity and permeability of wood absorb light, resulting in warm, embracing profiles. The user's sensation is that of flowing into the spaces, smoothly, without needing to adapt to access them. What Ispace manages to achieve is a synchrony between the signifier and the meaning, between the form and the mood of architectural representations, and those who live and perceive such content. It participates, therefore in the synchronization of conscious and unconscious interpretations of structures and proprioception in space that leads to a sensation of harmony with the world.

BUILDINGS WILL OUTLIVE US, SO WE BUILD FOR GENERATIONS TO COME.

The extension of structures across time and space creates a rhythmic, geometric and celebratory essence. Rhythm represents the brain's ability to interpret shapes in terms of repetitions and musicality, stemming from the physiological foundations laid by mirror neurons. Mirroring, indeed, extends beyond human interactions and actions; it encompasses emotions and sensations, connecting us not only with others but also with the world. Musicality encompasses and fosters harmony. The vibration emerging from the harmonious and rhythmic interplay of light and shadow projects deep significance into empty spaces. Emptiness in this context is not merely an unoccupied, static, and aesthetic space; rather, it is conceived as an extension of both body and soul.

Ispace assumes the role of a refuge, where the ritualistic and harmonious dimensions engage the user to a degree that transitions the bodily experience into a more abstract conceptualization. Shifting from a perspective that views the body merely as a physiological and anatomical structure, this process leads to the perception of a lived body[17] capable of experiencing emotions and comprehending the personal nature of received stimuli. This transformation occurs due to the presence of an atmosphere—a fusion of affective qualities defining a situation or space—enabling resonance through perception and full immersion in our surroundings. To reach this resonance it's necessary to conceive the structures as a collection of experiences, actions, sensations, and events intimately tied to those who inhabit these spaces. Not merely as a living body, anatomical in nature, but as a lived body, endowed with consciousness. An atmosphere cannot exist without the presence of a perceiving body.

Human interaction in space needs an emotional exchange, conceived as temporal corporeal firms, compositions of exteroceptive signals. The body starts to occupy the background of experience, becoming imperceptible. The body, initially the mirror of the external world, becomes the instrument through which we feel the world in an irreflexive way.

THE POWER OF ARCHITECTURE

Understanding the influential power of architecture on users' behaviors, subconscious processes, as well as their relationships and psychophysical health, is crucial for those designing spaces. It allows the reconnection of individuals with their inherent nature and a recalibration of the art of creation. The architectural experience influences our brains even before we interact with others or ourselves. Architectural encounters possess the ability to heal, amalgamate, and convey emotions. Architecture should confer dignity rather than taking it away. It should create an atmosphere that mediates between the mental and material dimensions. It should be human-centered: conceived for people, by people.

"In the fusion of place and soul, the soul is as much of a container of place as place is a container of soul, and both are susceptible to the same forces of destruction."[18]

THE ISPACES

Valentina Perazzolo

LOCATION:
ROSSA, GRAUBUNDEN, SWITZERLAND

Ispace is a project born out of the idea of combining art and architecture to create environments that stimulate people to perceive the influence of a given space on their moods. It is a re-evaluation of this mountainous territory, allowing a rediscovery of the bond with nature. Ispace is an invitation to discover paths through the valley that reveal the richness of biodiversity and the magic hidden in the forest.

CONSTRUCTION: JUNE 2023
SIZE: EIGHT STRUCTURES, EACH WITH AN APPROXIMATE AREA OF 20M^2
MATERIAL: LOCALLY HARVESTED LARCH TIMBER

The completed project will include ten timber pavilions built in the woods near Rossa in the Calanca Valley of Switzerland. The installation of the first work, which can also be likened to a sculpture, was completed in October 2020. From a design perspective, Ispace is a reflection on the role of architecture through a redefined, conscious approach that turns structural forms into tools for introspection. The project, undertaken by Davide Macullo Architects with the support of the RossArte Foundation, the municipality of Rossa, and the Swiss National Park Val Calanca has involved the inhabitants of the valley, visitors, and institutions, all working toward a common goal that contributes to the debate on the enhancement of rural areas. These installations/sculptures form part of the wider work of the Foundation, giving Rossa and the Val Calanca an identity as a destination for work and life, as well as tourism. Ispace is a territorial redevelopment project born from the social work, solidarity, and humanity of people of the region who are animated by the desire to bring life and culture to their place of residence and ultimately, to make the world a better place.

The work of Davide Macullo's studio is centered on the awareness that architecture is the link between the DNA of a place and its future. Macullo's series of drawings *Man seeking space* imagines the constant search to find the ideal space and scale to make visitors feel at ease. It is this idea that informs the architecture and has been translated into Ispace. People have the extraordinary ability to "feel" space with their eyes closed. The perception of space through the senses is central to the work of the studio, which began during Macullo's studies under Professor Luis Flotron in Lugano (SUPSI, 1987–89), who made the perception of space the focus of his research.

This intervention in the woods serves to provide a counterbalance to the trend toward the exponential development of technology that is altering the way humans build their habitat. The selection of a native material—larch trees cut on site on the slopes of the valley for the archaeological restoration of the ancient terraces—is a first sign of sensitivity to the environment and uses the material to the best of its evocative power. The purity of design thinking and the near absence of particular construction techniques brings to mind work that does not need to declare a temporal condition to emphasize the centrality of the relationship between humans and nature. The decision to simplify architecture to the utmost, creating small-scale sculptures with natural materials and placing them in nature, serves to evoke emotions without detracting from the essence of the architectural experience. These are, in fact, immersive sculptures that allow for interactions that spark emotions, memories, and visions.

SPHERE (SFERA)

The automatic mental connection made by the sphere with natural elements lies in the physical-chemical constitution of these elements themselves: the shallow, convex surface curvature is characteristic of living organisms, as it is naturally produced by the pressure of fluid from healthy tissue against external membranes. This "naturalness" and unconscious familiarity make anything that closely resembles nature inherently more attractive and pleasing on a perceptual level. This occurs because our brains may have evolved to process information about rounded shapes more efficiently, dedicating less cognitive processing to curved forms.

The reduction of static reference points and the sense of suspension due to the equidistance from the surfaces of the volume increases the sense of floating and detachment, similar to being in water. The Sphere is mentally associated with water and the color blue, which induces calm. Blue is generally related to relaxation and stress relief. Blue spaces, like green ones, evoke nature, allowing individuals who encounter them to engage in deeper introspection and reconnect with the natural world, which in turn fosters a sense of returning to their own nature as living beings. Generally, colors with earthy tones and undertones such as green, turquoise, and different shades of blue can raise a sense of relaxation, calm moods, and alleviate anxiety. Shapes have cross-modal correspondences, meaning that there are compatibility effects between their attributes creating stimuli across different senses. This phenomenon explains why we tend to associate certain shapes with specific colors, tastes, and sensations. People also tend to associate curved shapes with a sweet taste, a calm or soothing sound, a vanilla scent, a smooth texture, a feeling of relief, and a feminine quality. These associations can explain why, when entering the Sphere, we immediately feel at ease, and this comfort allows us to relax, and to communicate better with others and ourselves. The earth is our true home. Everything that belongs to it is instinctively and intimately familiar to us. To feel well, we need to connect with natural elements.

B
A

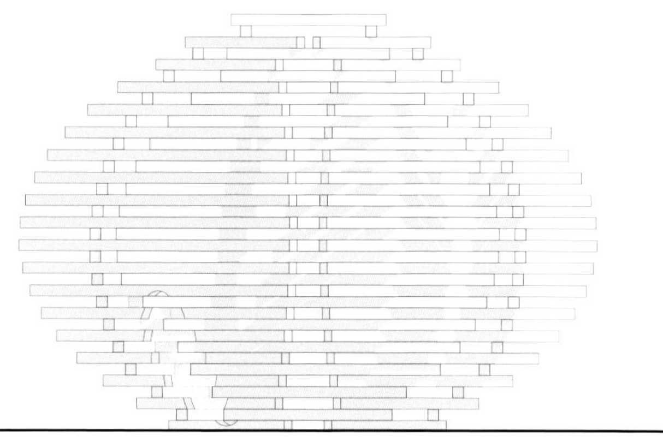

CUBE (CUBO)

The form of the cube is mentally associated with the earth and the color green. It evokes a sense of stability. Its conventional and familiar shape instills a protective, comforting feeling. It is strongly connected to the sense of gravity due to the verticality of its vertices, parallelism, and its rigid orthogonality. This familiarity is more social than instinctual. While the preference for spherical forms is rooted in biology, the preference for the cube has a distinctly cultural, social, and even physical basis.

The square is a familiar shape because it is deeply integrated in our daily and cultural experiences. Since the earliest human construction, such as homes, squares and rectangles have been used for their practicality and structural stability. These shapes, with right angles and parallel lines, have become symbols of order, balance, and security—qualities we associate with the stability of a home or an organized space. Additionally, the straight lines and symmetry of the square require less energy for the brain to process compared to more complex shapes. As a clear and easily recognizable form, the square evokes a sense of familiarity and predictability, qualities that tend to reduce anxiety and foster a sense of calm and security. The presence of a tree within it prompts reflection on the tree as a living entity. Moreover, stress reduction theories affirm that natural environments provide recovery from stress, while urban surroundings tend to hinder stress coping processes. Nature is also crucial to stimulate physical activity, social contact and cohesion, and, as such, it contributes to the achievement of well-being.

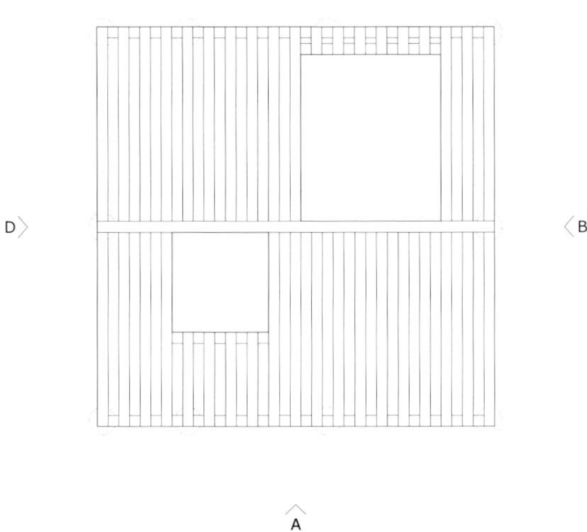

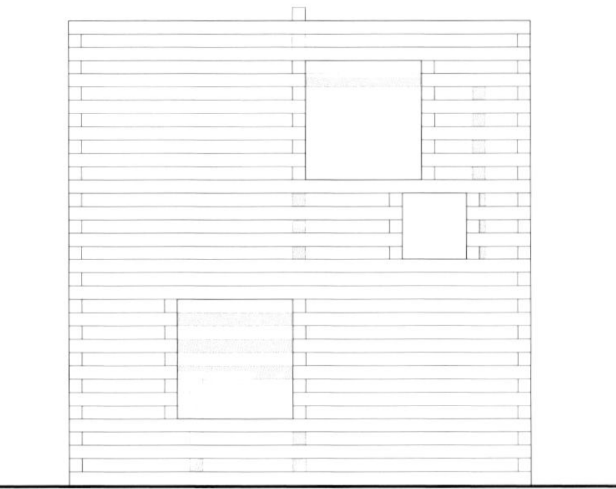

PYRAMID (PIRAMIDE)

The pyramid is associated with fire, the color red, and evokes a sense of aggression. The sharp edges, the obsessiveness of the triangular shape, the tension generated by a highly dynamic space, and the lack of an escape route increase the perception of anxiety and threat. Taking healthcare patients into account, for example, the color red is strictly connected with energy and encouragement, but at the same time it can lead to a sense of anxiety and overstimulation. From the literature, the arousal effect of red was documented by several studies measuring physiological responses. Kurt Goldstein, a professor of Clinical Neurology at Tufts, noted in 1942 that some Parkinson patients were observed while interacting with colors, and it was found that red had a tendency to worsen patients' pathological conditions, while green improved them.[19]

As mentioned earlier, certain attributes of shapes evoke compatible responses across different sensory modalities. Angular shapes are linked to sharp or sour tastes, dynamic sounds, and rough textures. These cross-modal associations allow our brains to create a more cohesive and intuitive perception of the world around us, aligning sensory information across sight, taste, touch, and emotion. What further contributes to the perception of threat and discomfort is the arrangement of the entrance. Unlike other shapes, a pyramid in this instance requires entry from below: one must bend and adapt their posture to fit the form, rather than the form adapting to them. This creates a sense of unease that is then reaffirmed and intensified upon entering and exploring the interior space. Similarly, the exit is obstructed by the limited—and uncomfortable—space, which constrains the path of escape.

C
B
A

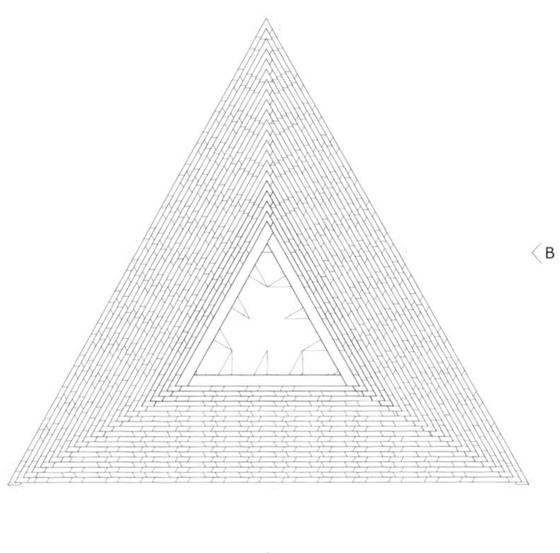

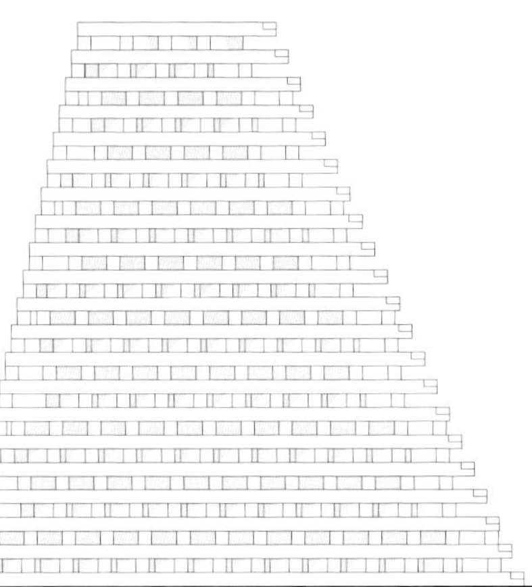

HOURGLASS (CLESSIDRA)

The shape of the hourglass is associated with air, the color yellow, and evokes a sense of freedom. The upward spiral invites one to break free from gravity and experience a sense of lightness, thanks to lines that are never parallel, extending perceptually toward the sky, and the air. The open view upward gives this sculpture a sense of verticality and spirituality, playing with the gentle contrast between the colors of wood, the forest, and the sky.

In a more symbolic sense, the hourglass also represents the opposing dualities of life and death, beginning and end, past and future. The three elements that condition human life are rhythm, space, and time. This shape evokes a feeling of flowing time and transience. Its symmetrical form, narrow in the center and wider at the ends, evokes balance and cyclicity.

The hourglass generates a sense of rhythm, musicality, and harmony. The spiral allows the viewer to grasp different aspects of the shape depending on the perspective and the light which creates a relaxing effect. On the contrary, bland and monotonous environments cause sensory deprivation and are detrimental to healing, since to maintain homeostasis (a psycho-physiological state in which the body maintains its functions in a stable and balanced manner) the brain needs constant but balanced change and stimulation.

C

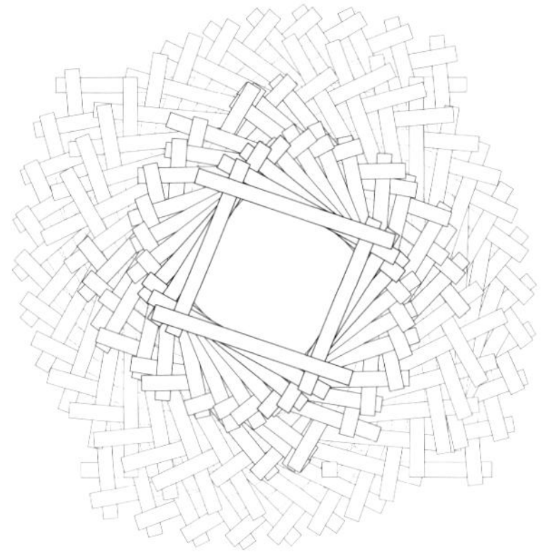

A

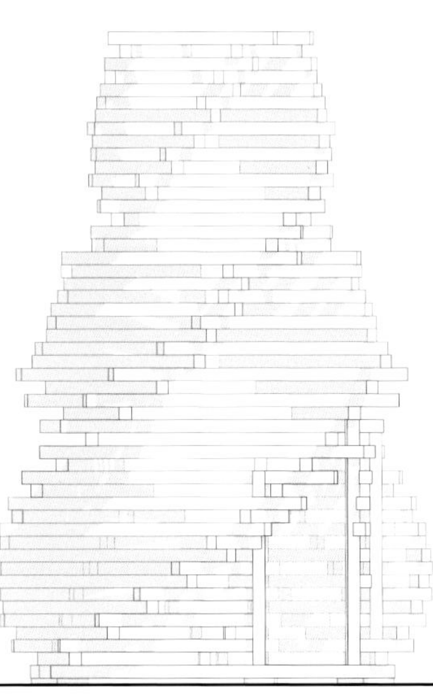

SPHERAMID (SFERAMIDE)

In this structure, the volumes of the sphere and the pyramid, associated respectively with water (blue) and fire (red), are mixed together. The structure thus unites two opposing sensations: the calmness of the sphere and the aggressness of the pyramid. The lines, converging at sharp angles to form rhomboid shapes, disturb the tranquility of the water element, creating a continuous dynamic opposition of fire and water.

Roger Ulrich's Stress Reduction Theory (SRT) posits that when people encounter an event or situation, they first perceive it in terms of its influence on their own well-being.[20] If an event is judged or appraised as harmful, threatening, or challenging, stress occurs usually accompanied by negative emotions. According to Ulrich, restoration derives from the reduction of stress, and exposure to nature can be a functional method to achieve this result. Biodiversity is also fundamental to sustain ecosystem processes and to generate well-being. It has positive effects on mental processes and behavior: psychological health, perceived restorative value, decreased depression, anger, aggression, increased self-esteem, reduced anxiety and tension, as well as increased vitality in children.

B
A

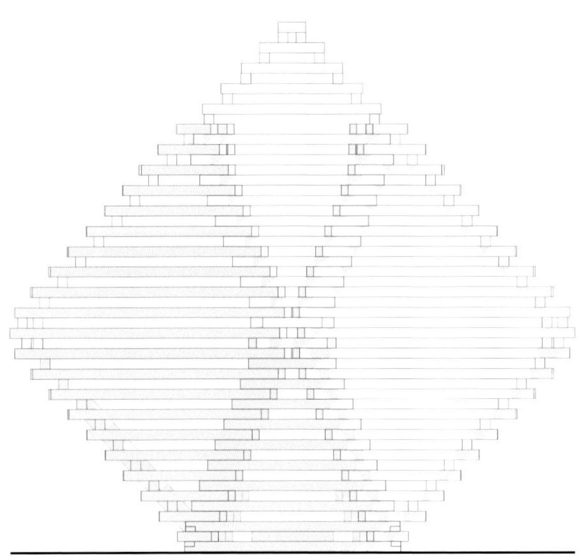

HOURSPHERE (CLESSISFERA)

The volumes of the sphere and the hourglass, associated respectively with water (blue) and air (yellow), are mixed here. This structure combines two sensations: the calmness of the sphere and the sense of freedom generated by the hourglass. The concave and convex walls evoke two contrasting sensations: introspective calmness, representing water, and dynamic propulsion, representing air. The contrast between open and closed shapes, and the dynamic energy directed inward and outward, gives the Hoursphere sculpture its power, evoking diverse sensations influenced by variables such as seasons, weather, mood, and more.

Before delving deeper into the shape's description, it is essential to highlight an important aspect of this creative process: the relativity inherent in the project. Perception of shapes generally depends on a variety of fluctuating or subjective factors. In this book, we aim to provide a baseline—a set of expectations about what we imagine most people will perceive and feel. However, interpretations of psychological reactions always rely on statistical tendencies rather than absolute values. While acknowledging the significance of individual variability— how each visitor, and even the same visitor at different moments of the day

or of his life, may experience Ispaces differently—it remains true that, especially for basic shapes, a significant majority of visitors have reported experiencing the emotions we sought to evoke.

The relativity of these feelings and reactions is influenced by factors such as the exposure to natural light. Natural light has been shown to significantly reduce negative emotional states, including anger, fear, confusion, mood swings, boredom, irritability, poor concentration, and sleep disturbances. Italian researchers identified strong correlations between exposure to natural light and psychological well-being during the pandemic lockdown in Italy.[21] This underscores the importance of integrating natural light and other biophilic elements into designs like the Hoursphere to enhance emotional and psychological outcomes.

Research also indicates that increased natural light is associated with enhanced serotonin[22] turnover in the brain, which correlates with a reduced incidence of anxiety, depression, panic attacks, and eating disorders. Additionally, its production rises significantly with greater sunlight exposure, particularly during sunnier seasons, thus underscoring light's role in mood regulation.[23]

C
D
B
A

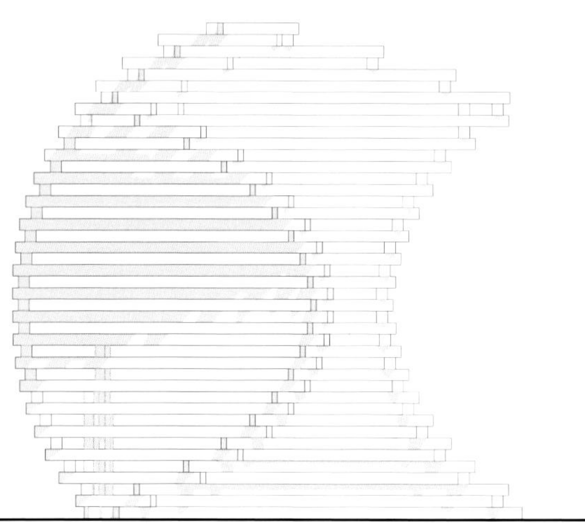

HOURAMID (CLESSIRAMIDE)

The volumes of the hourglass and the pyramid, associated respectively with air (yellow) and fire (red), are mixed together. This structure combines the dynamic sensations intrinsic to both. The lines converge in sinuous movements, like flames moved by air. The structure is dynamic yet repetitive and hierarchical, not instilling stability or calm. However, its dynamism helps counteract boredom, fatigue, lack of motivation, reduced attention, and the subsequent risk of disorientation. These effects are characteristic of monotonous environments, as demonstrated by research conducted in Canada[24] and in Brazil[25] that emphasized how monotonous settings can significantly impair cognitive performance and mood, further highlighting the importance of dynamic design in mitigating these effects.

The inability to see the sky makes the form an environment that, while not inhospitable, does not fully instill calm. It does stimulate curiosity and encourages introspection, giving a sense of protection on one side. On the other hand, it exacerbates the search for escape roots, making spatial orientation, a process driven by decision-making system, a potential source of stress. Good wayfinding helps maintaining stress levels low. The sound of the adjacent waterfall makes the experience even more immersive and powerful, emphasizing the presence of nature as a powerful and present force.

A

B

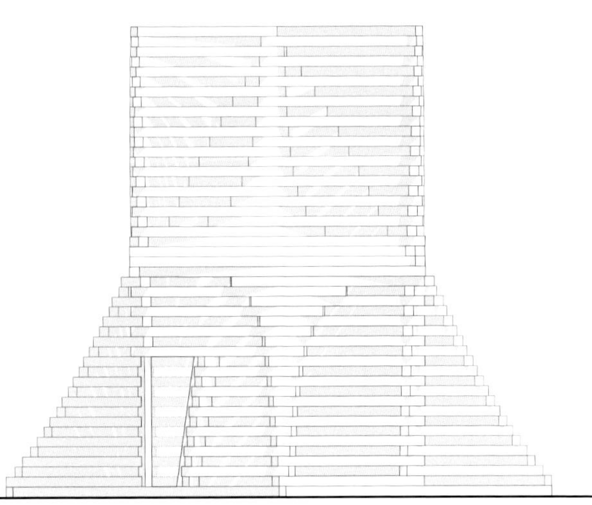

HOURCUPYRA (CLESSICUPIRA)

The volumes of the hourglass, cube, and pyramid, associated respectively with air (yellow), earth (green), and fire (red), are mixed together. This structure combines three sensations: the dynamism of air through the suspension of disjointed segments, the restlessness of fire and its threatening inhospitality, and the stability of the cube with its strong sense of gravity.

As with all sculptures, the use of natural materials decreases heart rate and sweating. It increases coherence, concentration, and memory retention. Overall, it enhances the sense of comfort and relaxation. Additionally, warm colors stimulate the senses. Wood, reintegrated into its natural environment, harmonizes perfectly with the context. Like the surrounding environment, its color and texture change depending on the season and weather conditions. With rain, it takes on a darker, cooler tone, while with sunlight, its essence and true hue prevail. Larch of course turns gray and eventually black over time precisely because of its exposure to sunlight and humidity.

Considering specific elements in design, natural materials appear to play a significant role in the cycle and quality of sleep, particularly in promoting recovery. In a 2003, a group of researchers observed that the heart rate at the beginning of sleep was significantly lower when participants rested in a stone pine bed compared to a decorative wood bed.[26] This finding suggests that the use of natural materials such as stone pine may positively influence physiological relaxation during sleep. Embracing biophilic interior design allows the creation of healthier, more energy-efficient spaces that might ultimately contribute to a more sustainable world.

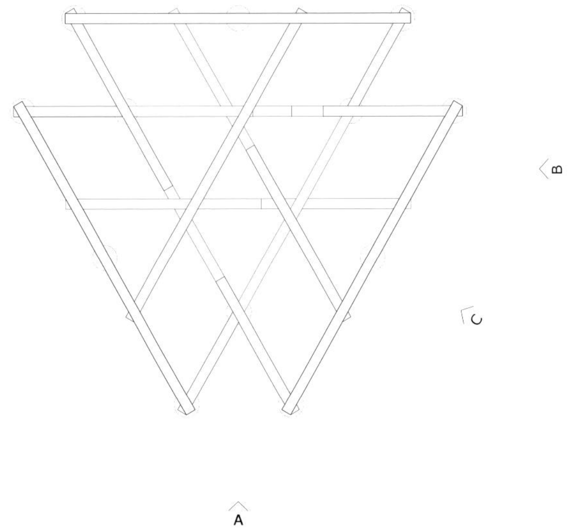

B
C
A

UNREALIZED ISPACES

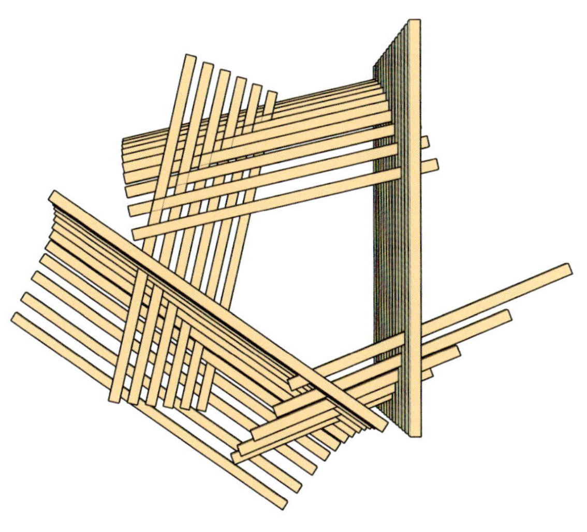

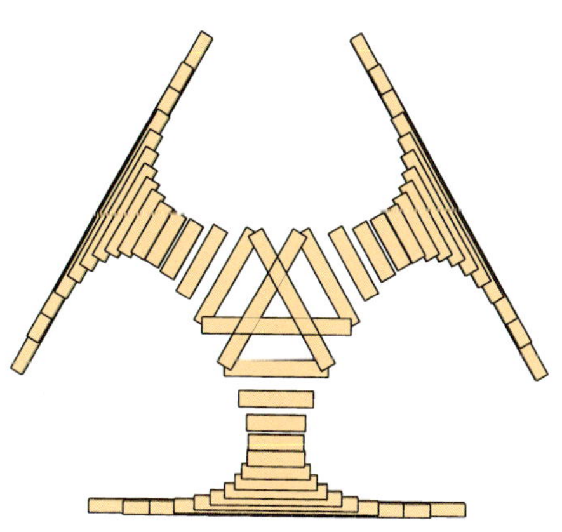

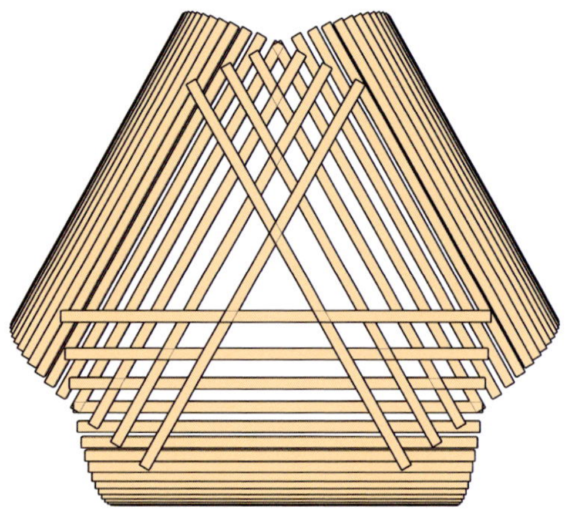

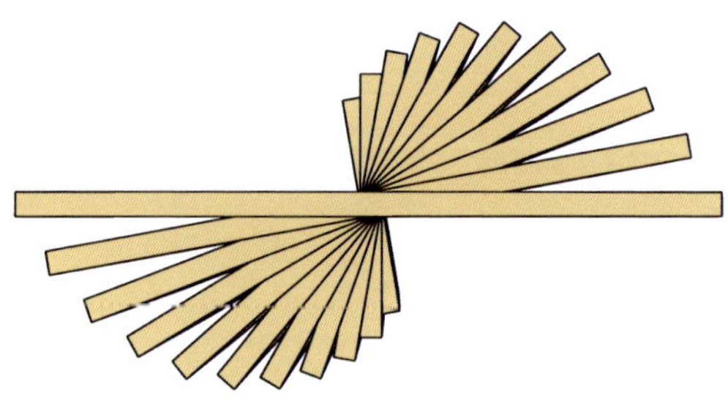

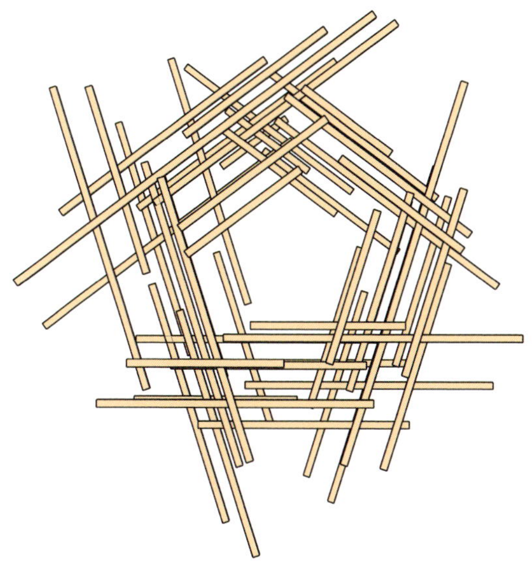

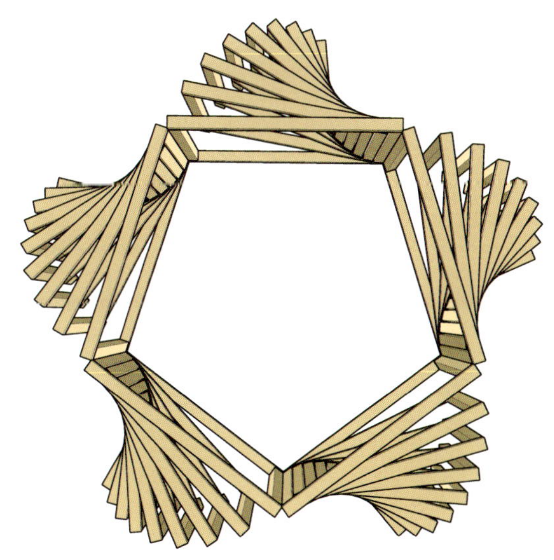

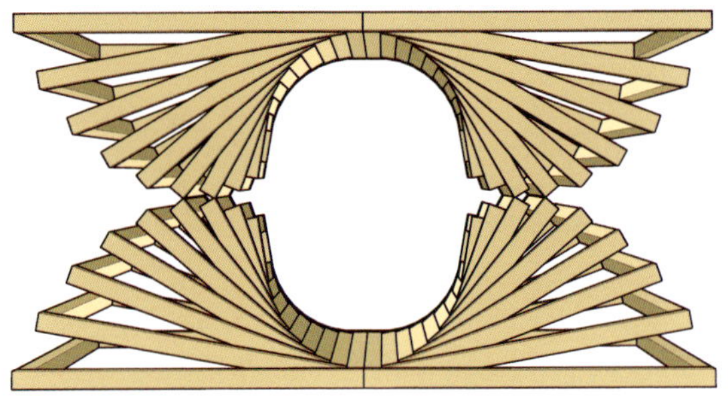

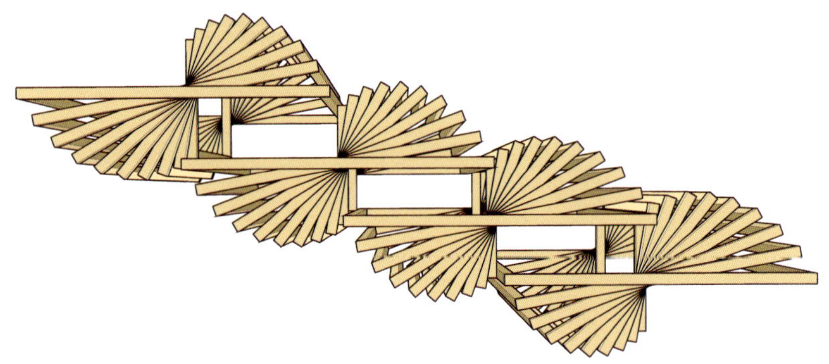

THE ROSSA PROJECT

The Swiss town of Rossa is located at an altitude of 1,100 meters above sea level in the Calanca Valley. It is thirty kilometers northeast of the city of Bellinzona in Ticino, but is in the Italian-speaking part of the Canton of Graubunden. Carved out by the Moesa River that finds its source near the San Bernardino Pass, the Val Calanca is accessible via a good mountain road that leads visitors into an unexpected and dramatic landscape, rich not only in scenery, but also in biodiversity. In 1683, the population of Rossa was 450 persons, however, continual emigration reversed only in the 21st century, left just 108 residents (and no children) living there in 1990. In the past fifteen years, the population has grown slightly and today there are approximately 160 inhabitants (and about ten children). Rossa, the highest village in the valley, initiated the restoration of its agricultural terraces and old settlement in the area known as Scata in 2012. This allowed for a comprehensive vision of the remnants of what was once a 16th-century Alpine settlement.

This village is the unexpected focus of the RossArte Foundation whose goal is to promote contemporary art and sustainable economic and cultural growth, thus "increasing the cultural public heritage of the Calanca Valley." RossArte was founded in 2017 by the Lugano architect Davide Macullo whose father was from Rossa, in collaboration with the town's mayor, Graziano Zanardi, the local urban planner Ivano Fasani, and the Italian gallery owner Mario Cristiani (Galleria Continua). Other participants have included the parish church, but also, significantly, residents of the valley who have been called on to express their opinions and to physically help with the work when appropriate. Additional collaborators include the Calanca Forestry Company, the Municipality of Rossa, the Val Calanca Park Association and the Regional Natural Park.

The Rossa Project includes numerous realizations including the Ispace pavilions described beginning on page 00, wall paintings on churches by David Tremlett, and a number of planned structures that will encourage the understanding and propagation of art in the valley. The architect's presence in Rossa is also marked by three houses he designed. The first of these was for his brother, and another for himself.

SWISSHOUSE I

Nearly twenty years before the creation of RossArte in 1998, Davide Macullo built the first project of his studio in Rossa. Swisshouse I, an 80m2 residence designed for his brother, is marked by two parallel concrete walls and a "floating" roof designed to echo local architecture. The architect explains, "The new volume is adapted to the landscape following the principles of traditional building construction. The size of the house, the internal and external spatial relationships, the dialogue between horizontal and vertical and the existing buildings of Rossa, recreate a spatial tension characteristic of this Alpine context; a tension that is balanced between stillness and motion." Swisshouse I clearly affirmed Macullo's desire to be respectful of the beauty of this place and its history, even as he dared to update and expand the architectural and artistic horizons of the Val Calanca. The three-level interior design also adopts the local, rural typology. On the basement level (traditionally reserved for the stable) there is the fitness area. On the ground floor, opening to the south-facing terrace, there are spaces for cooking and dining; with the sleeping areas on the upper floor. The architect states, "The interior space is open on all levels in order to provide an unobstructed diagonal view through the house and expands the perception of interior space. This is further emphasized by the longitudinal positioning of the stairs. The same principle is applied in the positioning of the openings, which in relation to the dimension of the interior spaces, are very generous in size. Through these openings and filtered by the loggia, the domestic space expands outward while the landscape is drawn inward." Provided with large openings and echoing the local combination of stone (concrete in this instance) and wood, the house succeeds in being at once modern and yet intimately connected to an old Alpine village. "Through this small project we have rediscovered the unique sensitivity and come to understand the reasons of the builders of the past," continues the architect. "Precisely because they had access only to limited resources, they chose to focus on the essential needs of living and on the relationship between man and nature."

The roof, in particular, recalls the traditional construction system of stone roofs, but is elevated by a series of galvanized steel beams and glass to emphasize its different function compared to the original uninsulated coverings. The house, in fact, ends with the walls, and the slopes covered with local stone become a significant and therefore sculptural element.

SWISSHOUSE XXXII

Completed the year of the creation of the RossArte Foundation (2017), Davide Macullo's residence in the village is called Swisshouse Rossa (XXXII). It has a total floor area of 300m2 and a generous volume of 1,000m3. The unusual painted timber facade of the house is a permanent in situ work called Sinusoïde created by the French artist Daniel Buren and in collaboration with Mario Cristiani. Although it has a reinforced concrete basement, the house is essentially built with local timber. With a plan in the form of a cross with rounded edges, the house develops an unexpected complexity, both from the exterior with Buren's colorful horizontal bands and inside where the main interior space rises in an overlapping and rotating series of articulated squares and rectangles. What is surprising is that Macullo and Buren succeed in integrating this decidedly contemporary house in the hold village in congruity not only with the neighboring buildings, but also with the mountain landscape that surrounds the village. A look up into Macullo's main living area seems to presage the rotating, rising forms of the Ispaces in the nearby forest, which were already in gestation. Davide Macullo explains that he involved Daniel Buren because "he taught us the pleasure of synthesis in observing the beauty of nature through his recognizable signs." The colors and even the forms of the house do not automatically harmonize with their environment, but the structure itself,

the way it is designed in wood are not at all the antithesis of local tradition. This is difficult to explain and even to show in images. One needs to walk through the village and to observe Swisshouse Rossa from various angles, to come upon it as what must be accepted as the harmonious presence of contemporary art and architecture.

The concept of the Rossa Art Project developed quickly beginning in 2017 with plans for a Hypogeum (underground) Sculpture House designed by the Engadine artist Not Vital. The planned space has a nearly cubic 3.9-meter-high top-lit main volume intended as a place to sleep and contemplate. Valentina Perazzolo, a researcher in "neuroscience applied to architectural design" who works with Davide Macullo explains, "We did not have the budget to build this project, but we intend to build it in the courtyard of the future youth hostel in the parish house, next to the main church. This may happen between 2026 and 2028." Vital, an unexpected artist born in Sent (GR) has a deep interest in architecture, as witnessed by his "Houses to Watch the Sunset," built in Tarasp (GR, 2018) and even beneath Palladio's dome in San Giorgio Maggiore (Venice, 2020). He also designed a house that can automatically be made to disappear into the hillside of his steeply sloped sculpture and architecture garden in Sent. "It's maybe like James Bond. Maybe poetic," he explained to the New York Times in 2013, "Into the womb."

SWISSHOUSE XXXV

Davide Macullo's third and most recent house in Rossa is called Swisshouse XXXV. Built for a private client, it was completed in December 2019. On a 391m2 site, the 70m2 house has a wooden frame finished on the outside with locally harvested larch timber, and inside with spruce. As the architect describes the project, "The volume is in dialogue with the vernacular buildings present in the village's nucleus, it takes on its forms and dimensions, but escapes an immediate perception, offering up continuous surprises with its dynamism extracted from a cubic matrix. The primary shape of the cube soothes us and makes us feel the gravity that keeps us firm to the earth, while its upward spiraling development breaks the symmetry and makes the space dynamic and light like the wings of a bird. This lightness that can be read from the inside in contrast with the external presence and enriches the experience of a journey that influences the moods of the inhabitants in positive terms, a sense of calm and freedom, underlined by unexpected views to the outside. The openings are oriented so that the surrounding landscape merges inside in a flow of nearness and distance, capturing the transformations of the environment given to us by natural light. A world of emotions in a minimal existential space." Macullo's references to the stability of the cubic form and the uplifting feeling of the rising spiral are again close to the psychologically driven shapes built in the nearby forests as part of the Ispace program.

FOUR CHAPELS AND A PAINTER

Born in 1945 in Cornwall, David Tremlett. A graduate of the Falmouth School of Art in Birmingham, and the Royal College of Art he has created a substantial reputation with his floor and wall paintings since the 1970s. Shortlisted for the Turner Prize in 1992, he completed the painting of the Capella del Barolo (La Morra, Piemonte, Italy, 1999) with Sol Lewitt, and more recently, City Drawing #1 in the lobby of the South Building of Norman Foster's Bloomberg European Headquarters in London (2017). On July 14, 2019, during the Feast of Our Lady of Mount Carmel, three "wall drawings" by Tremlett were inaugurated on historic local chapels in Rossa, at the initiative of the RossArte Foundation and with the unanimous consent of the parish assembly, funded by public and private institutions. In 2024, a fourth church was completed. Tremlett's bright, angular paintings now adorn the exterior facades of the Chapel of San Carlo al Sabbione (1686), the Chapel of Our Lady of Graces (1702), the Chapel of Santa Maria Maddalena al Calvario (1696), and the 17th century Pro de Leura Chapel. Painted directly on the walls of the chapels, the works become "sculptures" once they are completed, according to the artist. As these small structures stand out from their mountainous settings, in the spirit of Davide Macullo, they signal the fundamental compatibility of modern art not only with traditional architecture, but also with the powerful natural setting. As explained by the RossArte Foundation, "The opportunity to intervene so distinctively on historic buildings and artifacts is indeed a delicate matter that requires careful consideration for each specific situation, ensuring that the work is preserved rather than irreparably altered. The artistic intervention on the chapels in Rossa is undoubtedly bold and courageous, yet it allows for a clear distinction between contemporary elements and historic ones. The work is also potentially reversible, as the exterior finish of these buildings—particularly the paint—can be seen as a wear layer that is continuously changeable and renewable."

THE TEMPLE OF THOUGHT

Built in Rossa in 2023, the Temple of Thought set near La Scata "aspires to be the first place dedicated exclusively to man's ability to think. It is a place to sit. It is a place to stop even without thinking." There are now two other similar structures built with local workers and larch wood in Rossa, inspired by the form of the pinecone. The open form in which visitors can readily sit, has a diameter of about 130cm and a height of approximately 170cm—thus "relating to the scale of man," and perhaps also evoking the essential form of the egg. The second Temple of Thought is higher on the hill above Rossa, near the Chapel of Santa Maria Maddalena Al Calvario, one of the structures with wall paintings by David Tremlett. The third is on the opposite side of the Calancasca stream near the location of the Calancrok sculpture. Beyond these initial works, the architect and his team hope to inspire the construction of such small (between 2 and 9m2) structures in numerous locations. The project envisages the placement of the Temple of Thought in "public spaces around the world in order to emphasize the belonging to the human race of all, indiscriminately, beyond the diversity of cultural, religious, geographic, climatic, political, and economic environments." Indicative of the intellectually ambitious approach of Davide Macullo, the Temple of Thought evokes the potential for healing and introspection that can be inspired by a relatively simple architectural form. He says, "This embracing object intends to mark and physically signal the importance of devoting time to the preciousness of human thinking, to make us alert and aware that our quality of life, our survival and choice of priorities to follow in life, are linked to the quality of the thoughts we allow ourselves to elaborate. In each place, the material used for the construction of this temple-sculpture seat, will be chosen according to a sustainable and environmentally responsible approach." On August 23, 2023, a slightly larger structure of similar inspiration was completed in the woods near Tesserete promoted by the association Artinbosco (Ticino, Switzerland, near Lugano) and plans are underway for new structures in other countries in collaboration with artists and architects led by Maria Elena Rudolf and Florin Mindirigiu. The first reproduction of the temple abroad is the one in Tirana, Albania, completed in 2024.

The neuro-architect Valentina Perazzolo who works with Davide Macullo explains that the Temples of Thought are linked to "the desire to see similar sculptures emerge worldwide, each representing an element of the local environment and, of course, reflecting the freedom of expression of the artists, architects, or personalities involved in designing their own Temple of Thought." She emphasizes that, unlike the Ispaces, the intention of the Temple of Thought is to "embody the simplicity of thinking—a fundamental human capacity—expressed through an essential structure made of natural materials and shapes." The intention here is not to elicit psychological and physiological reactions but instead to stimulate free and open thought. The project also involves two figures from the worlds of art and architecture, the Swiss-Ecuadorian curator Maria Elena Rudolf and Florin Mindirigiu, the Romanian founder of the central and eastern European network (share-architects.com). Plans were underway to create Temples of Thought in Ecuador and Romania as this book went to press. The architects explain, "The Temple of Thought is also the ultimate synthesis of the studio's thinking: an architecture that constantly seeks nature in all its representations and uses humans as the primary measure. An architecture that wants to express itself through a coordination between arts, human sciences, and music in search for harmony with nature and the cosmos."

ART AND BOOKS

A number of art and architecture related projects have been planned in Rossa in coming years. Amongst these, the Art Village, Museum, and Camping area (2025/2030), is based in part on an idea developed by Le Corbusier and Pierre Jeanneret, the Musée à croissance illimitée (Museum of Unlimited Growth). Le Corbusier himself was an opponent of museums in the traditional sense, and this concept developed beginning with a 1931 letter to the editor of the Cahiers d'art. In that letter he detailed "a museum whose conditions would not be arbitrary, but which would, on the contrary follow the natural rules of growth in organic life, an element which could be added in harmony because the idea of the whole precedes the idea of the partie." Imagined as a timber structure with steel and concrete piles to protect the earth, Macullo describes his future museum as "a vision of redemption in terms of quality of life in a broad sense and cohesion through territorial stewardship. This focus is achieved through the commitment of local people and institutions united in creating what we call basic infrastructure. The project consists of a series of public interventions aimed at revaluing and rediscovering the territory, laying the foundation to motivate residents, in particular, to act as individuals supporting a sustainable economy that influences the region. As the first museum accessible 24-hours a day, it would take form as a "series of showcase pavilions set in a new park, visible from the outside, embodying the idea of indiscriminate access to art that permeates the entire Rossa project."

The Frott Bibliothèque and Events Hall (2025/2026) is another timber building with an approximate area of 200m2 that will include books about glaciers, art, architecture, local literature, and history as well as the digital archives of David Tremlett's work. This collection is to be curated by the Artphilein Foundation, created in 2006 in Lugano as a "non-profit organisation dedicated to contemporary art and photography." Referring in particular to the melting of the glaciers, Davide Macullo explains the purpose of the Hall in broader terms, "The Rossa project is to be read as a unitary initiative that strengthens existing heritage to affirm the desire for competitive growth on one hand and to act as a beacon of genuine intentions of the population shared with the other realities in the world. A room suitable for hosting work sessions to be shared with the population is a fundamental element for this growth and is a priority in territorial planning. The material produced during the sessions will form the cultural fund of the new Rossa archive, open to scholars and the general public."

The initiators of the Rossa Project have also imagined that the town and the valley could be ideal locations for temporary cultural events such as the Calanca Biennale, a 2021 outdoor exhibition that showcased 212 graphic works from fifty-six countries, selected from the 635 submitted for consideration. At the same time, Davide Macullo and the creative director of the 2021 Biennale Adria Nabekle created Calancrok, a twenty-five-meter long permanent sculpture made with thirty-two granite blocks cut in a local quarry with inscribed drawings made by local children during a workshop.

TO SLEEP, PERCHANCE TO DREAM

Given the expanding cultural horizon that Davide Macullo imagines for Rossa, places for visitors to stay are also essential. The old parish house in Rossa, which is part of the historic complex of the Church of San Bernardo (1677–84) is to be repurposed to accommodate young people and artists in residence. The project includes the construction of outdoor meeting spaces and a work studio. The roof of the building has already been renovated, and the actual project is ready to be implemented. A new hotel for visitors with sixteen rooms is planned for 2030 in the valley town of Augio about one kilometer from Rossa, and the existing Albergo Valbella in Rossa is being considered for a possible refurbishment.

Unexpected, in the spirit of the architect who is behind so much of this effort, the Rossa Project seeks new ways to develop the cultural and architectural presence of a valley that might otherwise have slowly been depopulated, despite its undeniable natural and historic wealth. With his family ties to Rossa and continued work there as an architect since the 1990s, Macullo is also a very cosmopolitan figure, having worked with the architect Mario Botta for many years and built extensively himself in Switzerland, Korea, Greece, Albania, and Italy. Others involved in the Rossa Project such as the founder of the Galleria Continua Mario Cristiani also have the kind of broad cultural horizon that makes these interventions in a

mountain town unusual. All the initiatives
in the Val Calanca share a respect for
the environment, for local history and
architecture, and view creativity in a
broad way that takes the psychological
aspects of art into account as seen in
the Ispaces. Rossa, as the highest village
in a relatively remote Alpine valley, is to
some extent isolated, which makes the
cultural initiative here possible in many
ways. Led by a person whose roots are
in the town, animated by others with a
broad and tolerant attitude, the Rossa
Project is above all supported and
encouraged by the local population,
surely an essential element of
its success.

THE ARCHITECTURE OF NECESSITY

Davide Macullo

Buildings will outlive us, so we build for generations to come. As Bruno Munari said, our journey is a time best used to contribute to allowing "a civilised people to live in the midst of their own art."

The architecture of necessity is a concept that covers every aspect of creating architecture. It offers the opportunity to organize thoughts, without necessarily finding or having to focus on a sequence of priorities. In creating a habitat, every element is considered, and, as such, can be instrumental in positively influencing a way of life. The two major themes we should consider in designing are the ecology of the Earth and human ecology.

Territory is the first essential element that building needs. The territory, our landscape, represents two prime conditions—the physical and the social—necessary for the transformation from a natural to a cultural condition. The first question, simple but fundamental is, "Why do I have to build in this place?" The place is never neutral and has unique and distinct values. The shift in positioning of a wall or an opening by even one meter changes both the meaning and the perception of an environment. The physical part includes climatic, geographical, orographic, geological, urban planning, and pre-existing conditions. The social aspect is constituted by cultural components such as history, traditions, social relations, the economy, and politics.

The task is to draw from the context until architecture becomes the link between the DNA of a place and its future. From a distance, a building is a form. The closer we come to it, it appears as a set of details filtering the outside and inside, and from inside it is a world, our world.

Our work is also imbued with a fundamental and universal value that is added to the specificities of a place: the psychology of the human being and the capacity for perception and assimilation of space through the senses and intellect. The analysis of these themes branches in many directions and leads to reflections that go deep into the ancestral needs of humans, the human condition—linked to a place—and future ambitions. It is a theme whose potential depends on the ability of the designer to question themselves through scientific, humanistic, and personal research. Fundamental to obtaining valid results are dedication through great curiosity, unconditional love for life, and the passion to draw from emotional states what is necessary to transform spaces into inhabit. These are the emotions that design spaces.

Every space reacts and influences moods, thus influencing lives. This is the greatest responsibility we assume in contributing to sustainable growth and to the human spirit. Building with respect of nature includes respecting human nature. The ultimate goal is to provide for a world where every individual can cultivate and better their being.

Unlike the past, both recent and remote, today the architect must take on a more humanistic role and relate differently to the technical field of the profession. Technology has exceeded the assimilatory capacity of a single individual, making building an increasingly interdisciplinary subject. It is good that the designer manages to direct the orchestra by focusing on the emotions of the sounds that feed and engage the audience.

Currently we are witnessing a general phenomenon, which leads people to experience spaces constructed in an increasingly two-dimensional way. This is due to a series of factors that have followed one another over time, starting with a more aseptic lifestyle, to the seemingly unstoppable increase in the concentration of populations in denser urban areas, and to the ease of rapid movement, which has increased in recent years.

The growing use of artificial intelligence, which unravels across the web of globalization, will result in an epochal change in the habits of the human race. We are close to complete robotization in in the capacity to create and print "not yet intelligent" buildings to be ordered online. These reflections lead to refine the role of the architect by choosing a possible evolution, which takes ecology into account in a broad sense. Even if today's spaces are realized in the laboratory, and tomorrow they will be realized in situ, the figure of the architect will be necessary to give a reason to build. We imagine a biodegradable fluid substance, which stiffens on contact with air and 3D printers that spray it on site to build our habitat by reacting to the surrounding environment according to a predefined schedule. We will have a complete project that will lack the poetic component of architecture, guided by human doubts and emotions. The limits of humans leads to obtaining sublime results because they are cultivated in the sphere of fragile souls.

To the universe of these ingredients that contribute to creating a project, we add others that we consider to be tools. Time is one of the fundamental tools for Gestalt, an organized whole that is greater than the sum of its parts. A building resembles a tree: roots-foundations, stem-structure, crown-spaces. We want a building to be an intuitive organism: one that becomes an extension of the senses, like having a long nose, enormous ears, eyes that see 3D, a huge mouth, and the longest limbs for the strongest embrace. Architecture must not require instructions to be lived in, but to offer a natural sense of orientation, to live in it simply by feeling at ease. Understanding the ebb and flow of human lifetimes creates the ability to make spaces static or dynamic based on their use, working on moods such as feelings of tranquility, aggression, fear, or safety.

The more reflections are articulated, reasoned, and sensitive, the more complete and continuous the experience is in living spaces.

A built place, like a natural one, must convey a sense of wonder in time—every day, but also with each passing year. This experience, linked to the expansion of time, brings us back to perceiving a place again in a complete way, no longer in two-dimensions only.

Human senses are the instrument of measuring surrounding space. The increase in technology leads to a slide in the use of perceptive functions. The task of the architect is, among other things, to take care of perception and stimulate people to "feel" embraced by harmonious spaces. The design is the connection of points, following priorities linked to contingencies on a three-dimensional grid like the stars in the sky.

In addition to the elements, the ingredients and the tools necessary for creation, there are other aspects that can be defined as the arteries of metabolic-space, comparable to the vital pathways of the human body and their structure that allow us to enjoy life in a positive way. One of these is to provide, for each environment, a visual escape route so that a person never feels trapped in a space. Another is to find the center of gravity of a composition that creates the feeling of psychophysical balance at every scale of the intervention, from the territorial to the intimate. This reflection starts from recognizing our body as a container of fluids that needs a continuous balance to calibrate our internal motion, avoiding excessive oscillations. The organization of spaces and spiral paths completes the perceptive experience of human well-being. The principle of structuring paths and spaces in a spiral motion allows for a sequence of time necessary for the individual to pass from a public condition to a private one, creating an intimate context wherein to cultivate dreams. Architecture must facilitate these harmonic steps to allow social cohesion based on mutual respect. Once we arrive in the most intimate space of a built organism, we find ourselves confronted with ourselves, and from there we can project ourselves into the universe.

Photo by Adriana Bertossa

DAVIDE MACULLO

Davide Macullo (b. Giornico, CH, 1965) lives and works in Lugano, Switzerland. Studied art, architecture, and interior design. For 20 years (1990–2010) he was project architect in the atelier of Mario Botta and was responsible for over 200 international projects. He opened his own atelier in 2000 and has since completed more than 800 projects in 49 countries. The ethos of the studio is "drawing from context," and the various contributions promote a dialogue between the specificity of the project and the universality of the contexts. The psychology of space orientation of the studio prioritizes human ecology and a conscious design approach that focuses on the power of space in raising emotions and connecting humans to nature.

LORENZA TALLARINI

AILEEN FORBES MUNNELLY

Lorenza Tallarini (1979, Switzerland) attended the Economic High School in Mendrisio and graduated in Architecture from SUPSI (University of Applied Sciences and Arts of Southern Switzerland) in Lugano in 2003. She joined Davide Macullo Architects in September 2006, where she currently serves as principal architect.

Aileen Forbes Munnelly (1977, Ireland) earned a degree in Psychology and a Master's in European Studies from University College, Dublin, before pursuing studies in Architecture (BA, BSc, March) at the University of Dundee. Since 2009, she has been part of Davide Macullo Architects, where she currently holds the position of principal architect.

ANDREA CARLOTTA CONTI

VALENTINA PERAZZOLO

Photo by Leonit Ibrahimi

Andrea Carlotta Conti (1995, Italy) studied at the Ezio Vanoni Technical Institute for Surveyors in Como and later earned a Bachelor of Arts in Architecture from SUPSI in Lugano. Since 2018, she has been working at Davide Macullo Architects, where she serves as senior architect.

Valentina Perazzolo (2000, Italy) graduated in psychology from the University of Milano-Bicocca in 2022, completing her final year at the University of Santiago de Compostela. She subsequently earned a Master's degree in Neuroscience Applied to Architectural Design from IUAV in Venice. Since 2024, she has been collaborating with Davide Macullo Architects, where she works as a neuroarchitect. For this book, she contributed to the writing of several texts and oversaw the editorial production.

Photo by Beny Steiner

PHILIP JODIDIO

Born in New Jersey, Philip Jodidio studied art history and economics at Harvard. In 1979, he became the Editor in Chief of the French monthly Connaisance des Arts, a position he held until 2002. A specialist in contemporary architecture, Philip Jodidio has published over 100 books including the Architecture Now! Series (Taschen), and monographs on such influential architects as Tadao Ando, Santiago Calatrava, Norman Foster, Zaha Hadid, Richard Meier, Alvaro Siza, and Renzo Piano. His body of work has served to bring contemporary architecture to the fuller attention of the general public in numerous countries.

NOTES

[1] Maurice Merleau-Ponty, Phénoménologie de la Perception, Gallimard, Paris, 1976. «C'est dans l'épreuve que je fais d'un corps explorateur voué aux choses et au monde, d'un sensible qui m'investit jusqu'au plus individuel de moi-même et m'attire aussitôt de la qualité à l'espace, de l'espace à la chose et de la chose à l'horizon des choses, c'est-à-dire à un monde déjà là, que se noue ma relation avec l'être».

[2] Intercorporeality: according to Merleau-Ponty this refers to the reciprocity of one's body and that of another.

[3] Simplexity: a neologism that suggests a complementary relationship between complexity and simplicity.

[4] Exteroceptive: activated by stimuli received by an organism from outside.

[5] Proprioception: a sense that provides information about the location of various parts of the body in relation to each other and the surroundings.

[6] The Fronto-Limbic System refers to a network of brain regions that play a crucial role in emotional processing and cognitive flexibility, particularly in the context of depression and its treatment.

[7] Affordances: physical features of an object that suggest how to interact with it.

[8] Peripersonal space (PPS) is defined as the space surrounding the body where that can reach or be reached by external entities.

[9] Epoche (from Greek and French words, usually without an accent in English): the act of refraining from any conclusion, or the suspension of judgement.

[10] Sensorimotor system: the connection between human perception and action that allows individuals to understand their environment and interact with it.

[11] Ideasthesia means "a union of sensations."

[12] Erwin Strauss (1891–1975) was a German and American phenomenologist and neurologist.

[13] Gestalt: a school of thought and a theory of perception that looks at the human mind and behavior as an organized whole that is more than the sum of its parts.

[14] Synesthesia is a neurological condition in which information meant to stimulate one sense stimulates several senses.

[15] The amygdala is a region of the brain primarily associated with emotional processes.

[16] Embodiment in architecture refers to the materialization of ideas, functions, and experiences into physical forms and spaces.

[17] Merleau-Ponty makes a distinction between the objective or physiological body and the lived body (corps vivant) which is experienced in a non-objective way.

[18] Robert Pogue Harrison, Gardens: An Essay on the Human Condition (Chicago: the University of Chicago Press, 2008), 130.

[19] Goldstein, K. (1942). Some experimental observations concerning the influence of colors on the function of the organism. American Journal of Physical Medicine and Rehabilitation, 21, June 1942, Issue 3, 135–93.

[20] Ulrich, R.S., Simons, R.F, Losito, B.D., E. Fiorito, E., M.A. Miles, M.A., M. Zelson, M. Stress recovery during exposure to natural and urban environments. Journal of Environmental Psychology, 11 (1991), 201–30.

[21] Spano, G., D'Este, M., Giannico, V., & colleagues. (2021). Association between indoor-outdoor green features and psychological health during the COVID-19 lockdown in Italy: A cross-sectional nationwide study. Frontiers in Public Health, 9, 751500.

[22] Serotonin is a neurotransmitter involved in regulating mood, sleep, appetite, and cognitive functions.

[23] Lambert, G. W., Reid, C., Kaye, D. M., Jennings, G. L., & Esler, M. D. (2002). Effect of sunlight and season on serotonin turnover in the brain. The Lancet, 360 (9348), 1840–1842.

[24] Thiffault, P., & Bergeron, J. (2003). Monotony of road environment and driver fatigue: A simulator study. Accident Analysis & Prevention, 35 (3), 383–94.

[25] Martins, L. B., Bezerra, L. F., & Vasconcelos de Melo, H. F. (2014). Effects of monotonous environments on cognitive attention and emotional well-being. Journal of Environmental Psychology, 38, 124–33.

[26] Grote, V., Lackner, H., Muhry, F., Trapp, M., & Moser, M. (2003). Evaluation of the effects of a stone pine environment on circulation, sleep, well-being, and vegetative regulation. Joanneum Research.